# The Keeper of Stories

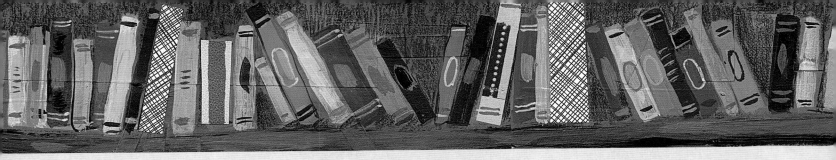

*For Gar Bear and KK, who helped me see myself as a keeper of stories*
*—C. K. P.*

*To my book club pals, keepers of many stories:*
*Shira, Minna, Barbara, Renanit, Harlene, and Jess*
*And to Karen Klein, an exceptional keeper of stories, too*
*—S. A.*

SIMON & SCHUSTER BOOKS FOR YOUNG READERS
An imprint of Simon & Schuster Children's Publishing Division
1230 Avenue of the Americas, New York, New York 10020
Text © 2025 by Caroline Kusin Pritchard
Illustration © 2025 by Selina Alko
Book design by Linn Laurent
All rights reserved, including the right of reproduction in whole or in part in any form.
SIMON & SCHUSTER BOOKS FOR YOUNG READERS and related marks are trademarks of Simon & Schuster, LLC.
For information about special discounts for bulk purchases, please contact
Simon & Schuster Special Sales at 1-866-506-1949 or business@simonandschuster.com.
The Simon & Schuster Speakers Bureau can bring authors to your live event. For more information or to book an event,
contact the Simon & Schuster Speakers Bureau at 1-866-248-3049 or visit our website at www.simonspeakers.com.
The text for this book was set in Adonis.
The illustrations for this book were rendered in acrylic paint, colored pencil, collage, and found objects.
Manufactured in China
0924 SCP
First Edition
2 4 6 8 10 9 7 5 3 1
Library of Congress Cataloging-in-Publication Data
Names: Pritchard, Caroline Kusin, author. | Alko, Selina, illustrator.
Title: The keeper of stories / Caroline Kusin Pritchard ; illustrated by Selina Alko.
Description: First edition. | New York : Simon & Schuster, 2025. | Includes bibliographical references. | Audience: Ages 4–8. | Audience:
Grades 2–3. | Summary: When a fire breaks out at the Jewish Theological Seminary library, helping hands from across the community rally together
to save the books and preserve the stories within the pages. Includes factual backmatter on the Jewish Theological Seminary fire of 1966.
Identifiers: LCCN 2023046375 (print) | LCCN 2023046376 (ebook) |
ISBN 9781665914970 (hardcover) | ISBN 9781665914987 (ebook)
Subjects: CYAC: Libraries—Fiction. | Fires—Fiction. | Jews—United States—Fiction. |
Community—Fiction. | Jewish Theological Seminary of America. Library—Fiction.
Classification: LCC PZ7.1.P7695 Ke 2025 (print) | LCC PZ7.1.P7695 (ebook) DDC [E]—dc23
LC record available at https://lccn.loc.gov/2023046375
LC ebook record available at https://lccn.loc.gov/2023046376

# The
# Keeper of Stories

Written by
## Caroline Kusin Pritchard

Illustrated by
## Selina Alko

### SIMON & SCHUSTER BOOKS FOR YOUNG READERS
NEW YORK   LONDON   TORONTO   SYDNEY   NEW DELHI

A library is
a keeper of stories.
A keeper of memories.
A keeper of hope.

This library, the one in the bustling college neighborhood of
New York City's Upper West Side, is a particularly good keeper.

Founded in 1893, this trusted keeper was one of
the biggest and proudest of its kind.

It held ten floors of tales from around the world
and back again.

They were the stories of the Jewish people,
precious stories of how their ancestors
sang
    and studied
        and feasted
           and faltered
              and prayed
                  and persisted.

Students and strangers, Jews and non-Jews alike, all flocked to the keeper, running their fingers across
the old

        the rare

              the sacred.

When others tried to erase these stories and their tellers, the keeper welcomed the words that were safe nowhere else.

But one April morning in 1966,
on a top floor of the peaceful tower,
a spark snarled into a twisted flame.
It wound up the single staircase and tore through the floor's metal grating.

One man, a maintenance worker, chased the burning smell.

But soon he was surrounded.

The tower transformed into a chimney, smoke bursting from its windows.

*Library walls, keep our stories alive.*

Alarms blared

      trucks raced

            ladders stretched

                  hoses filled.

The firefighters rescued the man inside,
but the books . . .
The books feared water as much as fire.
So the firefighters draped the shelves below as the flames crawled closer.

*Canvas blankets, keep our stories alive.*

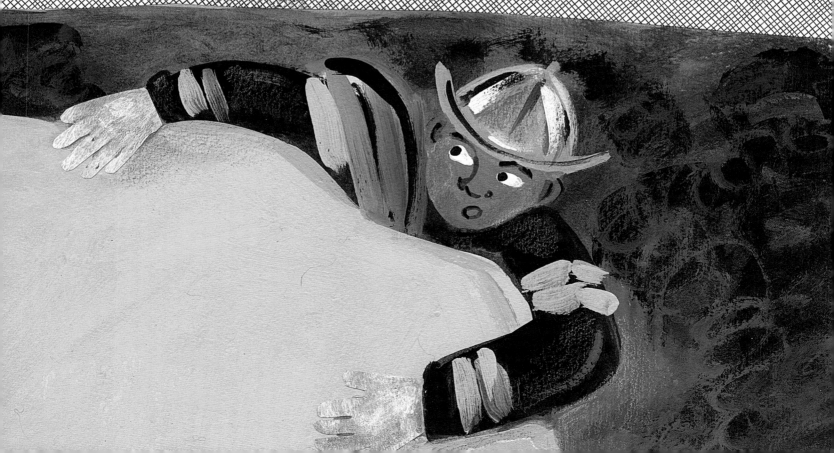

And then, the water surged.

It spilled past the Aramaic and Ancient Greek, the Yiddish and Ladino.
It tumbled through medical texts and medieval love stories.
It blasted over bindings, book after book.
It wrestled the fire until the sun sank behind the city's skyline.

*Rushing water, keep our stories alive.*

The next morning, people lined the streets:
*The books, the books,*
*what had happened to the books?*
Answers hung in the sour must.
The volumes on the highest floors
were now ash

ash

ash.

In the levels below,
    the books were bloated and warped . . . but whole.
    The charred shelves cradled hope
                                        hope
                            hope.
    *Swollen pages, keep our stories alive.*

The people looked up at the wounded building,
the one they had trusted for years.
They knew the truth.
That this keeper,
their keeper,
trusted them, too.
They couldn't let it down.

Hundreds of students and teachers, rabbis and pastors,
neighbors and strangers became "Operation Booklift."
They wound up the staircase like the flames had before,
forged together by stories.
Hand
      over hand
            over hand
                  over hand
they passed one drenched book down, then the next.
For two weeks, they lifted and reached, together.
An unbreakable human chain.
    ***Outstretched hands, keep our stories alive.***

Volunteers guided books from hands, to cartons, to wagons.
But with every minute that passed,
water turned dust to sludgy mud,
ink to smudged blots,
and pages to slimy mold.
They needed a plan—fast.

First, they placed books in every open nook across campus.

*Sheltering rooftops, keep our stories alive.*

But few pages dried, and those that did soon wrinkled.
They needed fresh air. . . .

The rabbi had an idea, one born from his childhood
cleaning books for Passover in the European breeze.
*Warming winds, keep our stories alive.*

But there was not enough room, and
the city's spring rain loomed.
They needed something bigger. . . .

A food scientist proposed a wild scheme: towering machines built for coffee beans rolled across town to freeze-dry the books.

*Vacuum pressure, keep our stories alive.*

But turning ice to vapor took time they did not have.
Too much longer and whole histories would be lost!
They needed a miracle. . . .

Finally, one volunteer presented a book to the rabbi.
A book layered with paper towels pressed between its pages.
A now dry, safe book.
And everything changed.

*Sheet after sheet, keep our stories alive.*

All they needed now . . .

were thousands of hands.

Journalists broadcast.
Merchants shipped.
Universities paused.

Students volunteered.
Kindergarteners baked.
New Yorkers unified.

Side by side, volunteers dried millions of pages.
Side by side, they
sang
          and studied
                    and feasted
                              and faltered
                                        and prayed
                                                  and persisted.

Side by side, they promised:

*You and me, we will keep our stories alive.*

Together, they saved 170,000 books and launched a new beginning.
Today, two new libraries later,
the
story
of
the
fire
still
lives
inside
every
stain,
rip,
and
wrinkle.

Yes, seventy thousand books were now ash.
*But our stories were not consumed.*

Languages were swallowed by fire.

*But our stories were not consumed.*

Torahs were buried.

But our stories
were not consumed.

Because the library is a keeper of these stories.
Because thousands of hands became keepers of these stories.
**Because *we* are the keepers of these stories too.**

Firefighters prepared hoses to put out the fire.

Smoke billowed out from two of the sixteen small windows in the library towers.

Books on the top floors were completely destroyed by the fire.

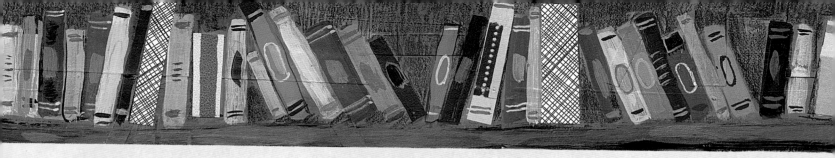

# The Jewish Theological Seminary Library Fire of 1966

The Jewish Theological Seminary has been a spiritual, intellectual, and communal heartbeat of Judaism for over 130 years. Its original library tower was ten floors high and held nearly 200,000 books, magazines, and newspapers dating back to the Middle Ages. It even held Torah scrolls from Danzig, Poland, which local leaders sent to the library for safekeeping before their town with nearly ten thousand Jews fell to total Nazi control.

On the morning of April 18, 1966, a fire broke out on one of the top floors of the library. Thirty-five fire companies from across New York City raced to the seminary. They fought the blaze for nine hours, with nearly seventy firefighters needing treatment for exhaustion and smoke inhalation. Seventy thousand books were completely destroyed, most located on the top three floors of the tower. Though they had escaped the horrors of World War II, the Torah scrolls of Danzig were lost in the fire, too. Following Jewish law and custom, seminary and community leaders came together to bury the remains of the scrolls in a nearby Jewish cemetery.

For two weeks, strangers came together in "Operation Booklift" to pass books down a human chain into cartons donated by delivery companies, which were then put on carts and temporary shelving provided by librarians across the city. The volunteers tried everything: standing the books up to dry across campus, spreading them out on the courtyard . . . even freeze-drying them with the help of General Foods scientists, engineers, and machines! What finally worked, though, was the process of "interleafing," which involved inserting a paper towel in between every two pages of a book, then repeating the process over and over again.

Thousands of volunteers returned and sat side by side to save an estimated 170,000 books with paper towels sent from manufacturers all over the city. Everyone played a role, even the preschoolers from the neighboring Riverside Church School, who raised $62.65 in a bake sale to help the rescue efforts!

Years before the fire, the seminary chose the biblical reference to the burning bush as their school's emblem. A sculpture depicting a blaze engulfing a bush was mounted on the very front of the library tower's entrance. It included words from the story of Moses in the wilderness: "And the bush was not consumed." For many, this story symbolizes survival, redemption, and the importance of faith. Just like the 170,000 books the community saved, the sculpture itself was not consumed by the library's catastrophic fire, and it continues to welcome learners of all backgrounds into the walls of the seminary to this day.

Volunteers spread books across the courtyard to dry in the breeze.

Volunteers of all ages and backgrounds manually dried books with paper towels.

Together, community members raced against the clock to recover books from the library tower.

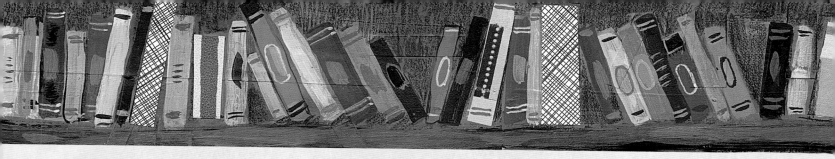

The Jewish Theological Seminary's library was rebuilt and stands tall today. It is home to some of the most celebrated Judaic studies manuscripts, rare materials, archives, and collections in the world.

# Author's Note

As I was thumbing through books in our congregation's library, I came across Barry D. Cytron's *Fire! The Library Is Burning*. It was my first time ever hearing about the 1966 fire at the Jewish Theological Seminary Library in New York City.

I began researching the catastrophe right as the COVID-19 pandemic was settling into every corner of our world. Schools and restaurants were shuttered. Masked strangers passed each other six feet apart on the sidewalk. Our political climate felt more divisive and isolating than ever. And yet here in these photographs from decades ago, I witnessed perfect strangers holding hands and passing books from one person to the next. I traced my fingers over images of neighbors sitting side by side in crowded rooms to save ancient, precious texts. They weren't just salvaging paper, of course. They were working together to fight for the very things that connect all of us: stories. This communal effort feels distinctly powerful—and rare—amid a proactive effort by many to ban books, particularly those with characters of color and LGBTQIA+ themes, from school and library shelves. I hope this story helps reveal our capacity for so much more than hate and fear-fueled censorship. If we see ourselves as keepers of stories, then we, too, must fight for their survival.

Just as Barry D. Cytron's book did for me, I hope this book that you are holding will help keep the memory of the fire alive. It is a story that reminds us of who we are at our core, and who we can never stop striving to become. To those at the Jewish Theological Seminary and all the strangers who came together to save our collective stories: May *your* story never be forgotten.

I am forever grateful to Dr. Menahem Schmelzer, the head librarian from 1964 to 1987, for sharing his own memories and wisdom with me, especially:

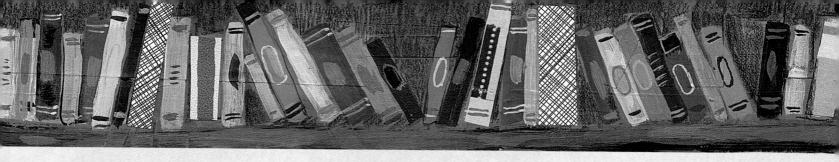

*"The precious value of old books that give us an insight into how people lived in the past and how people were creative in the past—that has to be preserved. Regular people from the community came together to help salvage the books. People from Harlem, from Manhattan, from all over formed this human chain up the library. The people thought of the books themselves, and they came together to save them."*

**Please go to carolinekusinpritchard.com to read the full interview.**

## Key Sources

Cytron, Barry D. *Fire! The Library Is Burning.* Minneapolis: Lerner Publishing Group, 1988.

Dicker, Herman. *Of Learning and Libraries: The Seminary Library at One Hundred.* New York: A Centennial Publication of the Jewish Theological Seminary of America, 1988.

Rabbi Menahem Schmelzer (head librarian at the Jewish Theological Seminary) in discussion with the author, October 17, 2020.

Rosen, Jonathan. "So It Is Written: Books Are Memory." *New York Times*, September 19, 2003. https://www.nytimes.com/2003/09/19/books/so-it-is-written-books-are-memory.html.

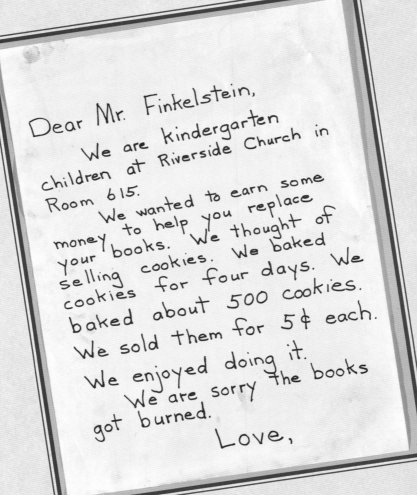

Dear Mr. Finkelstein,
    We are kindergarten children at Riverside Church in Room 615.
    We wanted to earn some money to help you replace your books. We thought of selling cookies. We baked cookies for four days. We baked about 500 cookies. We sold them for 5¢ each.
    We enjoyed doing it.
    We are sorry the books got burned.
                    Love,

A letter sent to and kept by the Jewish Theological Seminary from the 1966 kindergarten class of Riverside Church, whose bake sale raised funds to support recovery after the fire.

Class 615

MORIA
DANIEL
STEPHEN
MARGOT
PAGE
CURTIS
Wendy
JEFFREY
JOHN          CHRIS
kelly         ALAN
Susannah
MEGGY         MICAHEL
POLLY
FREDA         TIMOTHY
Ichiro        IAN
MARIE CHRISTINE
CHRIS POPE LUCAS